[

MW00467365

"For Your Marriage"
"12 Tips for Building a Godly Marriage"

Written by Pastor/Evangelist Chuck L Turner Sr.

Edited by Joanne Turner-Jordan

Cover design by The Prophet X

I dedicate this book to my mother Florence Lee Turner, the strongest woman I know. Also to my beautiful wife LaVenise Young Turner who has stood by my side through thick and thin. Also my children Cyndal M. Turner, the one who makes my heart smile, Chuck L. Turner Jr., and Devon A. Turner. I would also like to thank Pastor Sonny and Sister Julie Arguinzoni the founders of Victory Outreach International, one of the greatest ministries in the world, for their love, kindness, and example throughout the years. Special thanks to Pastor/Elder David Martinez (R.I.P.) and Sister Faith Martinez my spiritual mom and dad without whose help I wouldn't be who I am today. Also thank you to Pastor Augie Barajas and Sister Mary Barajas for their influence in my life when I returned to California. Also thank you to my current Pastor Michael Gonzalez and his wife Sister Christina Gonzalez for not only encouraging me but allowing me to pursue what God has called me to do. And finally thank you to the many Pastors all over the world who have graciously allowed me the privilege of standing behind their pulpits to minister the word of God as I have treasured each and every opportunity!

Pastor/Evangelist Chuck L Turner Sr.

All scripture references are from the New King James Version of the bible.

Introduction

After growing up running the streets of Altadena/Pasadena and becoming addicted to crack cocaine, Pastor Chuck Turner gave his life to the Lord in 1987 during his stay at the Men's Recovery Home in Victory Outreach of the San Fernando Valley. He then served for 17 years under the direction and leadership of Pastor/Elder David Martinez. After attending Bible School Pastor Chuck became a licensed minister with Victory Outreach International in 1993 and served in the local church (VOSFV) as an Associate Pastor, Marriage Counselor, Worship Leader, Choir Director, Bible School Instructor, and Recovery Home Director. In 1999 after hearing the call of God Pastor Chuck began ministering as an Evangelist, singing and preaching in many churches across the United States. There was a challenge given to him in 2004 to take over a small struggling church in Washington, DC and Pastor Chuck accepted. He then served from November 2004 through October 2012 as Senior Pastor of Victory Outreach Washington, DC. After sensing the leading of the Holy Spirit to return to the Evangelistic field he returned to California. From October 2012 until July 2015 he served as an International Evangelist with Victory Outreach Eagle Rock as his home church, under the leadership of Senior Pastor/International Prayer Leader Augie Barajas. While in Eagle Rock Pastor Chuck also lead a Bible Study for married couples. In August 2015 Pastor Chuck, along with his wife and daughter relocated to Palmdale, California and is presently serving as an Associate Pastor/International Evangelist with Victory Outreach Palmdale as his home church under the leadership of Pastor Michael Gonzalez. Pastor Chuck Turner has been with his wife LaVenise Turner for 39 years, (29 years married), they have three children, Cyndal Turner, Chuck Turner Jr., and Devon Turner. Over the years he has sang and preached at many churches throughout the United States, also in Europe and New Zealand. Pastor Chuck has recorded three separate musical projects and been privileged to sing at many conferences and conventions, as well as acting and singing in several musical productions with Victory Outreach International. He was also granted the opportunity to speak at the Victory Outreach World Conference in 2005 at the Long Beach Convention Center. From the East Coast to the West Coast and many places in between as well as abroad, God has used his life to win souls and strengthen the saints for the work of the kingdom!

Preface

What can be said about marriage that hasn't already been said? Well hopefully there are a few things that can yet be discovered about the institution of marriage. When you take into consideration that we all possess our own unique individuality, it tells me that no two marriages are exactly alike. With that in mind I believe there are no standard answers to the problems many married couples face. It is not my intention to provide solutions for every couple who struggles to find marital harmony. It is however my intention to speak to those couples whose specific situations line up with the teaching and message of this book. There will undoubtedly be many couples who can benefit from this book and perhaps see substantial improvement in their relationships.

The question that will arise for some people will be, "What qualifies you to write a book about marriage?" While I cannot boast of having a degree in clinical science or a degree in counseling or a wall full of acronyms, (i.e. PHD, MD, BA, etc.) what I do possess is experience! Don't misunderstand me, anyone in possession of those degrees or certificates are to be given the utmost respect for their knowledge and achievements. It speaks to the depth and substance of their educational background. Having said that I still believe that there is no substitute for experience especially when it is based on success in a given area. What I do have is 29 years of successful marriage.

What I can also say is that there has been no infidelity during those years nor has there been a physical altercation on any level. My children have never witnessed a fight between me and my wife. Not so much because we've hidden it from them but because they rarely occur and when they do they're never explosive outbursts of anger. In addition to my personal experience in marriage I have also attended and taught Bible School. I have over 25 years of ministry experience. I have served as a Marriage Counselor/Associate Pastor as well as speaking at several Marriage Seminars. I became a licensed Minister in 1993 and have worked with many married couples at various levels over the years. I served as leader of a Married Couples Bible Study for 3 years in addition to serving as a Senior Pastor for 8 years in Washington D.C.

With all that being said I'm still learning what it means to be a good husband and father. But I'm confident that I have a lot to give to this subject and it would be a crime for me to go to the grave without sharing what I know to be valuable insight for someone's marriage. I've always said that knowledge comes from books, (and I've read my fair share) but wisdom comes from experience and observation. It must be stated that the distance between what we learn and what we apply can be as wide as the ocean or as thin as paper depending on the level of commitment we bring to the table. So what I've experienced in my own marriage combined with what I've observed in the marriages of others has armed me with great weapons to defeat the enemy whose goal it is to destroy families!

Regardless of what type of background you have, whether its drug addiction, or domestic violence, or a dysfunctional family (by the way whose family is functional?), it could be all or none of those things and this book can still be an asset to your life and marriage. If you believe that God brought you and your spouse together then you must also believe that it is your **Destiny** to have a happy marriage. I pray that this book can help you to summons the **Courage** you need to make the necessary changes that will ultimately bring you the happiness you seek.

So this is it, **Destiny & Courage, For Your Marriage!** I pray that it helps you to cooperate with God in the building of a successful marriage!

Destiny & Courage
"For Your Marriage"
"12 Tips for Building a Godly Marriage"

By Pastor/Evangelist Chuck L. Turner Sr.

Chapter One
In the Presence of God and These Witnesses

It seems only fitting that we begin this book with scripture from the beginning of the one book that is at the heart of everything I believe to be helpful for a successful marriage. That book of course is the bible. In Genesis 2:18 it says, *"And the Lord God said, It is not good that man should be alone; I will make him a helper comparable to him."* Then in verses 21-24 it says, *"And the Lord caused a deep sleep to fall on Adam, and he slept; and He took one of his ribs, and closed up the flesh in its place. Then the rib which the Lord God had taken from the man He made into a woman, and He brought her to the man. And Adam said: 'This is now bone of my bones and flesh of my flesh; she shall be called Woman, because she was taken out of Man.' Therefore a man shall leave his father and mother and be joined to his wife, and they shall become one flesh."* It must also be added that Jesus said in Matthew 19:6, "So then, they are no longer two but one flesh. Therefore what God has joined together, let not man separate." It is on the foundation of these truths that I intend to speak about the great institution of marriage.

If one can accept that marriage was born in the heart of God and that it was designed to be a lifelong commitment then one can begin moving along a path that will lead them to that end. The truth of God's word can serve as an adhesive when times are tough. Sadly divorce has become all too common in society today, both in Christianity and in the secular world. While there is much debate about the increase or decrease of divorce from a statistical standpoint, I don't believe anyone can argue that it's perhaps more acceptable today than in times past. The Huffington Post shared an article dated December 2, 2014 that says, "The truth about the divorce rate is surprisingly optimistic." The article offers statistical evidence that suggests couples are marrying at a later age than in times past. It says that the more mature couples are staying married more often than the couples who marry much younger.

The data sounds encouraging except that it doesn't mention that there are fewer marriages than there were in the past. More couples today are cohabitating or "shacking up" which would have an impact on those numbers. Those couples who "shack up" are enjoying the benefits of marriage without the commitment. In the U.S. most states will give them the common law marriage status after seven years which only seems to matter when there is a break-up and money or property is involved. What I'm saying is that there are many divorce/break-ups that probably didn't factor into their equation. So maybe it's not the 50% number that's so often thrown around. Perhaps it's 40%, or 30%, or even far less!

None of those numbers matter at all if your marriage is struggling! The bottom line is the divorce rate could be going down everywhere except in your own household! So let's throw out all the numbers and talk about the pain of an ailing marriage and what the Lord can use as medicine to ease that pain and ultimately heal a marriage. Before we move any further into possible solutions or answers let's take a look at the commitments we made through the vows we made on the day of our weddings. I realize that nowadays many couples are writing their own wedding vows and so the wording can be arranged in a variety of ways. I want to examine the traditional wedding vows because I believe that all wedding vows are theoretically attempting to accomplish the same goal and that is a lifelong relationship.

The following vows are taken from "The Pastor's Handbook" produced by Moody Publishers:
(To the bride/groom)_____(bride/groom's name), wilt thou have this man/woman to be thy wedded husband/wife, to live together after God's ordinance in the holy estate of matrimony? Wilt thou love him/her, comfort him/her, honor and keep him/her, in sickness and in health, and forsaking others, keep thee only unto him/her, so long as you both shall live? (The normal response is "I will")
(To the bride/groom) Repeat after me. I, _____ (bride/groom's name), take thee, _____ (bride/groom's name), to be my wedded husband/wife, to have and to hold from this day forward, for better, for worse, for richer, for poorer, in sickness and in health, to love and to cherish, till death do us part, according to God's holy ordinance, and thereto do I give thee my pledge.

Of course the vows don't have to be in any specific order or vernacular but these are most likely the more familiar. I believe far too often couples recite their vows perhaps routinely or mechanically and somehow devalue the power and importance of the words spoken on their wedding day. The fact that God planned for marriage to last a lifetime is evident in the scriptures. Jesus says in Matthew 19:8, *"Moses, because of the hardness of your hearts, permitted you to divorce your wives, but from the beginning it was not so."* That verse intimates that it was the unwillingness of people to be forgiving, or understanding, or loving, or compassionate, or have empathy toward their spouse that precipitated the decision to allow divorce. Or put simply, it was their inability to honor their vows.

This is not groundbreaking or earth-shattering news but it should at the very least cause us to examine our hearts and see where we are in our level of commitment to our mates. When you consider that to be a Christian means to be Christ-like, then there should be a conviction about not bearing the fruit of the Spirit in our marital relationships. I've found that on far too many occasions it has been easier for me to bear the fruit of the Spirit with others than it has been with my wife. I'm not sure what the psychology is behind that thinking but I do know that I tend to work harder at being on my best behavior when I'm away from home. I generally feel far less inhibited when I'm around my family and that can sometimes lead to an unhealthy attitude. I've observed in several cases particularly in church where people will extend the love of Christ to others more readily than they will to their own spouse. And believe me when that becomes habitual your mate will notice and take exception to it. Galatians 5:22-23 says, *"But the fruit of the Spirit is love, joy, peace, longsuffering, kindness, goodness, faithfulness, gentleness, self control. Against such there is no law.*

My relationship with my wife took a dramatic turn for the good when I started to work at applying these verses to our marriage. Things in my household were made a lot easier when the Lord showed me that the stability of my relationship with my wife is more important than winning an argument. That revelation inspired me to pursue the fruit of the Spirit in our marriage and experience the blessings that resulted from that decision. I decided to take responsibility for the condition of my marriage and lead the way in making peace. Matthew 5:9 says, *"Blessed are the peacemakers, for they shall be called the sons of God."* The way I see it, if I initiate the process of peace in my household there is a blessing that awaits me. Therefore I choose to be on the front end of the peacemaking process and not on the back end.

I have to remember that I promised to love, comfort, honor and keep her regardless of the condition of her health. I also promised to maintain fidelity in my marriage. I also publicly declared that for better or for worse, for richer or for poorer, my commitment would be till death do us part. That, my friend, doesn't happen without a lot of changing, and compromising in ways that are mutually beneficial so that you can keep your promises. No marriage succeeds based solely on what is said and done on the day of the wedding. It's a lifetime of learning to be flexible for the sake of love. There are a variety of things that make flexibility a constant need in marriage. As time goes by we all change as children come into the picture, as we age and change physically, sometimes even health can deteriorate as we get older. Being flexible makes it possible for us to change with the changes and maintain a stable relationship regardless of what happens.

I included the marriage vows so that we could be reminded of the seriousness of what we promised to fulfill in the life of our spouses. As we continue to examine what makes for a good marriage, I pray your heart is open to receive what could possibly revolutionize your relationship with your spouse. So whether you're just starting out or if you've been at it for several years God can still do a miracle in your marriage and heal the wounds of your past and present so you can have a bright future. You and I need to see God's **Destiny** for our marriages and have the **Courage** to work toward that end.

Chapter Two
For Better or For Worse
Embracing Both Ends of the Spectrum

I must confess that on far too many occasions I've made verbal commitments without taking into consideration the total amount of effort needed to make good on them. I'm sure you've experienced it before. Those times when you've volunteered to help someone with something while having in your mind that it will only require a minimal amount of energy to fulfill what you're now obligated to because you said you would do it. What I've discovered is that people will more often than not withhold critical pieces of information regarding exactly how much help they need for fear that it will negatively influence your decision to assist them. For example someone asks for help with moving from one place to another. There are two things you can pretty much guarantee you're going to hear. One is, "The place I'm moving to isn't that far away." Two is, "I don't have that much stuff; it'll be easy." If you believe either one of those things I have a bridge I'd like to sell you. First of all, their idea of close is probably not what you had in mind. And secondly, everybody has a lot of stuff! I've found myself grumbling my way through several moving jobs saying things like, "She said it was close! The other place is clear across town!" Or, "They said the packing was almost done! They're not even 50% packed!" Or maybe it was, "This is way more stuff than I thought it would be! We're gonna be here all day!" Or how about this one, "I wish they would've told me the apartment they're moving into was on the third floor and there's no elevator!"

These illustrations may sound a bit nightmarish but anyone who's been involved in helping friends move have encountered at least some of these and possibly a few I didn't mention. The point being that for better or for worse we're now obligated to see it through regardless of how we feel because we gave our word. Sometimes a marriage can be kind of like that moving job. You don't know how far you may have to go to please your spouse and possibly they didn't expose you to 100% of the baggage they brought into the relationship. Personally I like cruising along during those "For Better" times. Marriage is easy when everything is going well. It's during those times when we get fooled into thinking we've finally got this marriage thing figured out. You know it's those seasons when you've got all your ducks in a row so to speak. Financially, you've got no problems. Things have been going really well at your job. All the bills are being paid on time. You haven't had a money draining emergency in months! From an intimacy standpoint, things couldn't be better! You and your spouse are enjoying regular date nights. Your sexual experiences have been awesome and with regularity! Your wife hasn't had a headache in months! Your husband has been giving you a lot more attention lately. (Which actually coincides with the fact that football season is over.) The arguing and fighting over small things seems to have disappeared. Even the children are behaving. Basically you're enjoying a storybook marriage. You get the feeling that says, "We're going to live happily ever after!"

Okay, I know I kind of over did it with some of those things but you get the picture. The "For Better" is what every couple wants and it's what every couple is prepared to experience. Let me reiterate, I love the "For Better" seasons in my marriage. It's during those times that my wife and I have built some incredible memories. Great times on vacation! Great times with our children! Great times in ministry! But the reality is those times don't last forever. I've come to accept that just like there are "For Better" times, there are also "For Worse" times. I'm sure that like most people I entered into my marriage totally unprepared to encounter the "For Worse" aspect of our lives together. Jesus says in Matthew 5:45, *"that you may be sons of your Father in heaven, for He makes His sun rise on the evil and on the good, and sends rain on the just and the unjust.*

As I've matured over the years, I came to the realization that it isn't the "For Better" I need to be prepared for, it's the "For Worse!" It's safe to say that "For Better" is a welcome guest in our home that we hope will stay as long as he wishes. However, "For Worse" is that person we never invite to any of our parties but somehow they manage to show up anyway and ruin everything. It can be described as those times when financial disaster strikes perhaps in the form of a layoff or an unexpected expense that throws your finances into chaos! Or it can be the result of a bad investment or purchase that forces you to live outside your means. If you, or your spouse, are high maintenance personalities this can have a devastating effect on your relationship. We'll talk more about that in a later chapter. The "For Worse" season can also be the result of physiological changes that can negatively impact the intimacy between a husband and wife. Particularly for women as they mature and experience menopause. Believe it or not ladies, even men can sometimes have seasons where they are not as motivated as they would normally be. It could be the result of lower testosterone levels that are part of aging. Or it could be due to weight gain by either party that could make them initially seem less desirable.

Let's face it if you're around my age (fifty?) or older, you're just not the same person you were when you were younger. That doesn't mean your marriage has seen its best days, it just means you adjust accordingly and still enjoy each other's company. This can also be a time when one or both parties involved can become irritable and therefore arguments start much easier. Sometimes this can happen because secretly the husband blames the wife for what's happening, while the wife secretly blames the husband for what's happening. Without humility, understanding, and healthy dialogue, this season can be extended by our own stubbornness.

One other thing I'd like to touch on about the "For Worse" season is the loss of a loved one. Especially, if that loved one was a primary-family member. A primary-family member would be a child, a parent, or a sibling. Different people cope with loss in different ways. Just because your spouse is a Christian doesn't automatically mean they can expedite the grieving process. There's no standard timetable for grief. There's also no way to know what other areas of a person's life will be affected by their grieving. If you are in this season or have been in it, be compassionate, be understanding, give your mate the time and space they need to process their emotions, and love them through it. I've counseled with couples who've struggled during this season of their marriage. Sometimes one person loses patience with their partner because their grief has impacted the intimacy in the relationship and even subjected them to the emotional ups and downs that come without warning. This is a season when prayer, the word of God, and the fellowship of the saints is the best medicine.

The good news is that "trouble don't last always!" Hold on my brother! Hold on my sister! Because the "For Better" is just around the corner! Remember that part of our vows when we said, "For better or for worse" which probably should say, "For better and for worse" because we encounter them both on this marriage journey. Do everything in your power to live in the "For Better" season of your marriage for as long as humanly possible but be prepared spiritually and psychologically for the "For Worse" seasons. My wife and I have known each other for 39 years and we've had more "For Better" than we've had "For Worse" but we've had to learn how to navigate through both ends of the spectrum. God's plan for your marriage is that your life be made better by the person He has given to walk with you through this life. It's up to each one of us to do what we can to make our mates life better by how we cooperate with them to fulfill the will of God. We can achieve that by being prepared for whatever life throws our way! Tell your husband/wife today, "For better or for worse, I'm gonna love you baby! No matter what comes our way! We're gonna make it!"

Chapter Three
Love and Respect
Ephesians 5:22-33

The Apostle Paul under the divine inspiration of the Holy Spirit had a lot to say about marriage. It's rather interesting that God would use a single man to teach about this subject. That's one of the many things I love about God, He chooses the most unlikely candidates to carry out His work. (You can include me in that list of unlikely candidates!) Ephesians chapter five includes one of the more popular passages in scripture used to teach on marriage. Interestingly at the conclusion of these passages he states that he's talking about Christ and the church, however it is very much applicable to married couples. He begins his discourse in verse 22-23 by saying, *"Wives, submit to your own husbands, as to the Lord. For the husband is the head of the wife, as also Christ is the head of the church; and He is the Savior of the body."* He goes on to say in verse 25, *"Husbands, love your wives, just as Christ loved the church and gave Himself for her."* If we skip down to the end of these passages in verses 32-33 the Apostle Paul concludes by saying, *"This is a great mystery, but I speak concerning Christ and the church. Nevertheless let each one of you in particular so love his own wife as himself, and let the wife see that she respects her husband."* So the Apostle Paul makes it clear in verse 33 that the key message he was looking to communicate concerning marriage was that of love and respect. These are two actions that can without question go a long way in stimulating a healthy marriage.

It's beautiful to see how God through His word speaks so accurately about the psychology of men and women long before there were marriage counselors or psychologists. Our Creator has and always will be the foremost authority on what makes us tick! Over the years I've either taught or attended several marriage seminars or classes in which we participated in one of those exercises where the men and women are asked to list their five most important needs in marriage, prioritizing them from one to five. In almost every situation the women listed love or romance as their number one need. Conversely, the men more often than not listed respect or sex as their number one need. I'm sure that most of you who are reading this book have been a part of something similar to or exactly like what I just described. There would always be laughter as we considered how differently men and women generally think. For example, women listed love and romance, without necessarily thinking sex. Men listed sex, while thinking about love and romance. Most of us men had to be educated on the difference between the two. However the great majority of men had respect as a high priority on their list of things they needed most in marriage.

So it would seem that God had it right all along and He used the Apostle Paul to communicate a truth that most married couples can benefit from. The primary need for the wife is love while the primary need for the husband is respect. I said most married couples because there are no absolutes when it comes to something like this. There will always be that individual who is the exception to the rule but by and large these truths will most often be applicable. If we can accept this as fact and not just conjecture then we must move in a direction that would see us infusing these actions into our relationships. So if you're a husband it begs the question, "How do I love my wife?" The short answer is, "like Christ loved the church!" Obviously, we're going to need a little bit more than the short answer.

Throughout the bible, the analogy of marriage is used to describe the relationship between Christ and the church. The church is often referred to as the bride of Christ. In Revelation 19:9 it speaks of being called *"to the marriage supper of the Lamb!"* In His parable about the wise and foolish virgins, (Matt. 25:1-13) Jesus uses a wedding as the backdrop of His teaching about the end times. So then our marriages are to be a reflection of the love relationship between Christ and the church. Let's examine the relationship between Christ and the church to better understand what God is asking us to do as husbands

First of all Christ was born into the world for the church. In other words they were made for each other or meant to be together if you will. As a husband you must come to terms with the fact that your spouse was made especially for you. There is within your marriage the capacity for the two of you to become lifelong soul-mates. The fact that God ordained for the two of you to be together can be rendered useless by ignorance or unbelief in His divine order for your life. Just because you and your mate were handpicked to be a pair doesn't mean you won't have to nurture and care for your relationship to keep it healthy and growing. What is does mean is that no matter what challenges you face if you put your trust in God He will see you through! Lastly, if you can accept this as truth for your marriage it makes fidelity the logical choice.

The second aspect of the relationship between Christ and the church is summed up in the word sacrifice. Jesus laid down His life for the church! This is an area that throughout the years has been particularly challenging for me because I tend to be selfish. I'm certain that there are millions of men and women who suffer from this very same character flaw. Simply put sacrifice means "the act of giving up something that you want to keep especially in order to get or do something else or to help someone." (Merriam-Webster) I have on a number of occasions been guilty of having a "me first" attitude even with my wife. It shows up in areas of my life where it's usually unnoticeable to others. For example if I stop at a fast food restaurant and get burgers and fries for me and my wife I generally make sure to keep the bag so I can get all the fries that fall to the bottom because I don't want her to have more. If we share a sandwich and I have to cut it in half, I will carefully inspect both halves to make sure mine is bigger. Those things may seem small and insignificant but they're a part of a much larger problem that is my selfishness or unwillingness to sacrifice.

Of course, the sacrifice Jesus made was His own life! Having said that, I am in no way trying to compare what Jesus did to French fries and sandwiches! And yes I do know that it speaks more about selfishness and not sacrifice. You may not like my illustrations but when you think about it isn't selfishness the number one hindrance to sacrifice? The selfish person will never live sacrificially! The point I'm trying to get at is that in order for me to love my wife sacrificially there are things in me that need to die. I suppose one could say, "C'mon Pastor it's only French fries and sandwiches!" Those who would say that help to make my point. If it's such a small and unimportant issue, why would you be unwilling to change it? Remember the wisdom of the Song of Solomon 2:15, *"Catch us the foxes, the little foxes that spoil the vines."* You and I as husbands need to find those small unnoticeable character flaws and bring them to the altar of sacrifice and allow them to die for the sake of our marriage.

Finally, the relationship between Christ and the church is driven by His unconditional or Agape love! This means that as a husband I am challenged to give my wife an unlimited supply of love, forgiveness, grace, and mercy. One of the things I appreciate about cell phone contracts these days is that most of them include unlimited minutes for talking. That feature affords me the privilege to call as many people as I want during any billing period without fear of being charged for overages. The cell phone company is saying to me, "It doesn't matter how much you call I'm going to treat you the same. I won't charge you any differently." Unfortunately, in marriage many times when we place limits on the amount of love, forgiveness, grace, or mercy, our spouses get charged for overages. It shows up when we decide to withhold any of those things for any reason. Unconditional love could also be described as unlimited! It's like the lyrics from the Jesus Culture song "One thing Remains" says, "Your love never fails. Never gives up. Never runs out on me!" Unlimited love will produce forgiveness! Most Christians see grace and mercy as the same but they're not. Grace gives us what we don't deserve, while mercy keeps us from getting what we do deserve. Or look at it like this, grace gets us into heaven and mercy keeps us out of hell!

The bottom line is if we as husbands give our wives what they need most they will give us what we need most, which leads me to my next point, and that deals with the wife giving her husband respect. Typically we give respect to individuals we believe to be superior to us either in authority, in finance, or in intellect. Even if the wife exceeds her husband intellectually and/or financially, she must still respect his God given position as the head. In Joshua 3:7 the bible says, (And the Lord said to Joshua, *"This day I will begin to exalt you in the sight of all Israel, that they may know that, as I was with Moses, so I will be with you."*) While this doesn't speak about marriage, it does speak about God's desire for us to see His people they way He sees them. The word says that God exalted Joshua in the sight of Israel so they would give him the same respect they gave Moses. When God says that the husband is the head of the wife, He is exalting him so that she would give him respect. I could also say that Joshua appears in these passages as a type of Christ leading Israel who is symbolic of the church, so the relationship between Christ and the church is illustrated which is the basis for the entire teaching on marriage.

In this day and age, it is not uncommon for the wife to be the bread winner in the family which can for some women lead to a prideful attitude toward their husband. But the wife's respect for her husband shouldn't be based on his financial status but on his God-given position as the head. Even when the wife's educational accomplishments exceed the husbands, she would still be wise to consult with her husband regarding decision making out of respect. Those things will go a long way in building his self-esteem and affirming him as a husband. A wife should also not be contentious or argumentative. Proverbs 21:19 says, *"It is better to dwell in the wilderness, than with a contentious and an angry woman."* I would advise for the wife to refrain from being a scorekeeper or a mind reader. Scorekeepers keep track of every detail of daily life in terms of who contributes the most to household chores or to the children, or who apologizes the most, or who is most often in the wrong. They see their relationship with the sense that one person is winning and one is losing.

Obviously, this behavior can be detrimental to building a strong marriage because it is divisive and it conflicts with the concept of the two becoming one. It promotes a mentality of individualism rather than a team mentality which is the more productive mindset. The acronym T.E.A.M. (Together Everyone Accomplishes More) isn't only applicable to church and business it works pretty well with marriage and family also. Mind-readers are often undone by their own propensity to function based on assumptions. When their anger boils over in a given situation they generally respond by saying, "He or She should've known!" or "He or She knew exactly what they were doing!" In most cases the injured party has never made their feelings known regarding the issue in question. They're not only guilty of attempting to read their spouses minds, they're guilty of expecting their spouse to read their minds as well. I can tell you from experience that mind-reading in a marriage is a bad practice that only contributes to a problematic relationship. I would be remiss if I didn't mention that husbands can also be guilty of practicing this behavior. The key to avoiding this pitfall is communication. When couples are free to communicate their feelings openly and honestly mind-reading becomes a thing of the past. So if your husband/wife is behaving in ways that you're unhappy about its best that you communicate your feelings about it and eliminate the problem so you won't be inclined to mind-read.

Chapter Four
Agreements
Amos 3:3 *"Can two walk together, unless they are agreed?"*
(NKJV)

This is one of the most simple, yet powerful attributes of married life that often gets overlooked. When it really gets down to it this is what being married is all about! On our wedding day when we said our vows weren't we in fact making an agreement to honor what was spoken in the presence of those who witnessed it? Most importantly, in the presence of Almighty God! And to a lesser degree, those in attendance. Regardless of where those vows were spoken, whether at a church, in someone's backyard, or in a courtroom, they still carry the same weight.

Every agreement gets tested over time. Especially in business we see agreements that seemed fair in the beginning reach a point where the parties involved want to renegotiate. Financial agreements often have to be re-visited when they've existed over long periods of time because of inflation and the rising cost of living. In those types of situations the agreement can lose its effectiveness and make it difficult to honor it as it was originally stated. For example, if someone agreed to work for $1,500.00 per month in the 1970's it would at that time have been a good deal. Gasoline was less than a dollar a gallon. Houses were selling for around twenty thousand dollars or less in the inner-cities. Apartments were renting for around $400.00 per month. You certainly wouldn't be rich but you could get by. However that same agreement would look way out of proportion here in 2016! Gasoline is almost three dollars per gallon. (At least now it is!) Houses are now selling for around three hundred thousand dollars in the inner-cities, in some places a lot more than that! And you'd be hard pressed to find an apartment for less than $1,000.00 per month!

The uniqueness of the marriage agreement is that it can't be renegotiated! That agreement is like God, it's the same yesterday, today, and forever! The wedding vows represent one huge agreement we enter into with our spouse. The power of the words spoken on our wedding day doesn't diminish over time. They are as potent and powerful today as they were when first spoken! But that agreement by itself won't sustain us through the ups and downs of day to day living. What then becomes necessary are smaller agreements that serve to support the larger one. Because what can two people do together without first agreeing? The answer is nothing! We can't even walk to the corner store together unless we first agree about the destination. Perhaps you like CVS Pharmacy, but she likes Rite Aid or Walgreens or maybe Walmart! The point is even something as small and seemingly insignificant as that can become a bone of contention between two people.

What's the solution? We support the main lifelong agreement with a lot of smaller agreements that are needed for successful daily life. If we can come to an agreement about things like money, children, household chores, sex, leisure, giving, and a host of other things relevant to our everyday lives, we can have a happy and thriving marriage. Time will test the vows we made but if we use those smaller agreements properly they will strengthen the marriage so it doesn't collapse. One thing is for certain, we can't argue about something we agree on! It only makes sense that we should agree about either having children or how to raise them. About family money, how much to spend, how much to save. To help clarify this point I've included the following diagram: (The large outer circle represents our marriage vows, while the smaller inner circles represent day to day agreements necessary for co-existing peacefully.)

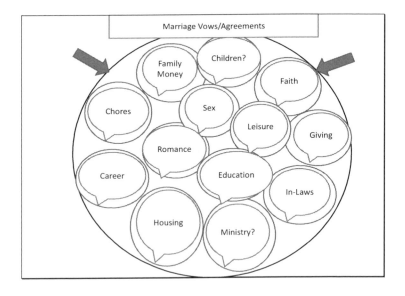

The great thing about these agreements is that they can be renegotiated over time. These smaller arrangements can be altered as life changes. For instance, laws have changed over the years regarding child discipline which can make raising children an issue that needs to be re-visited. Age and or health concerns could impact our sex life and make it necessary to come to a new agreement on how much and how often. The loss of a job could have an effect on the original agreement about family money and facilitate the need to re-evaluate that arrangement. And at any given time the call of God could affect how we feel about our ministry involvement. Should the in-laws have input in your marriage? How much? How little? Or not at all! (Personally I'd recommend the latter.)

What should be obvious is that like the prophet Amos said, *"Can two walk together, unless they are agreed?"* The answer is, no they can't! God has called us as married couples to walk through this life together till death do us part. And the vows we made on our wedding day aren't sufficient to solve the problems we face during our day to day struggles. Communication, negotiation, and yes a little compromise here and there is what it takes to have a successful and happy marriage. Over these last few years as I've given myself to full-time ministry it has lead me to take a more active role in the kitchen while my wife works. It was easy for me to reach that agreement with my wife because it was the right thing to do. Has my decision for full-time ministry limited us financially? Yes it has! But we've agreed to wait on the Lord for our breakthrough!

Every step of the way I've strived to apply this to our marriage and as a result I have reaped the benefits of a peaceful household. I challenge you to examine your relationship with your spouse and see what you argue about.

Once you identify those areas then you can begin to one by one come to an agreement with your mate about how to handle it moving forward. Everything you agree on is one less thing to argue about! And in the event you have to agree to disagree, do yourself a favor and avoid that subject as much as possible.

Chapter Five
Distractions
The Subtle Seduction of Social Media/The Heroes of Hollywood

When we talk about marriage and what makes it successful there's no way that the subject of communication doesn't arise at some point in the discussion. I have never had a counseling session with a couple in which they didn't list communication as one of their problems. In my own marriage when it comes to keeping the lines of communication open and flowing in a healthy manner, sometimes I do a good job, other times not so much. That's probably true with most couples if they're honest. What I've noticed that seems more prevalent in this high tech age we live in today is most of us carry our own distraction around with us in our pocket or our purses. That distraction is what is commonly referred to as a cell phone. The cell phone has become a major hindrance to healthy communication in many marriages today. Don't get me wrong I don't know what I would do without it! Twenty-five years ago most of us saw it as a bit of a luxury. Today we all see it as a necessity! The cell phone has become ingrained into not just American culture, but every culture. The evolution of the cell phone into what we now call a smart phone or android is nothing more than a pocket computer with the capability to make calls or send messages via text. The fact that almost everyone can access the internet with their cell phone has made the entire world available with just one touch.

So the question is what impact has this had on the marriage relationship? In my humble opinion, it has become a major distraction. I suggest that we as a society have been seduced by the power and influence of social media. And that seduction has found its way into the life of many married couples today. Couples today can find themselves communicating more with their Facebook friends than with their own spouse. Our phones are now being inundated with opportunities to add new apps that will ultimately serve to create even more distractions. There is Facebook, Instagram, Snapchat, (also a host of others I'm unfamiliar with) and a plethora of games to keep you focused something other than what's most important. I recall about a year ago me and my wife went out for dinner. Much to my chagrin I have to admit we spent more time looking at our phones than we did talking to each other. It's as though I've become addicted to my cell phone and its notifications. There are people who claim bragging rights based on who has the most Facebook friends. I get several friend requests daily and some of them from people who are not the kind of friends I need. On several occasions I've received friend requests from women trying to lure me into the world of pornography and I know I'm not the only one. Now my distraction has evolved to become a temptation! Praise God for the power to overcome temptation!

But many husbands are not living with the indwelling power of the Holy Spirit and are victimized by the enemy. Proverbs 1:10 says, *"My son, if sinners entice you, do not consent."* One of the other notifications I've received is when my phone tells me someone poked me. C'mon people are you serious? What possible reason could there be for getting poked? I never know exactly how I'm supposed to respond to it so I generally ignore it. It just feels like another avenue through which I can be distracted by my phone. Posting pictures and various things on Facebook or Instagram can also invite a lot of positive reinforcement from outside of the marriage that may or may not be helpful. We must be careful with some of the comments we receive from people we don't even know. I'm not suggesting that social media is evil but it has the potential to be if it's left unchecked. I use social media to promote my Evangelistic Ministry most of the time but I also use it to stay in touch with friends and family. I believe the key is having a purpose or vision for how you plan to use it because that will help you establish boundaries. Proverbs 29:18 says, *"Where there is no revelation (vision), the people cast off restraint."* Without a clear vision or purpose there's no specific goal. Without a specific goal there are no guidelines necessary. When we have a clear objective we restrain ourselves against anything that would obstruct us from achieving it. The truth is we can fall into the trap of giving more attention to social media than we do to our spouse. Be careful with social media because its seduction is very subtle.

Another distraction that can invade many marriages comes from the Heroes of Hollywood. With the popularity of talk shows and their charismatic hosts as well as the so called "Reality Shows" more and more people are getting their world views from the television. Even Christians are having their faith watered down by the opinions expressed by some of their favorite celebrities. In some cases Dr. Phil, Oprah Winfrey, Steve Harvey and many others have greater influence in people's lives than the word of God. Oftentimes these so called experts are challenging the word of God and teaching that Christianity as we know it is outdated and old fashioned. In this age of political correctness having a biblical view on life has become exceedingly unpopular with the voices of Hollywood.

Probably just as significant is the casual approach to honoring the marriage vows modeled by Hollywood couples. It seems that in many instances celebrities either marry several times or are engaged in pre-marital sex, or sex outside of the marriage. There are many behaviors that are projected as normal that must be rejected by the believer. Not only is the Hollywood image of marriage questionable but also the physical appearance of those we see can lead to the pressure to achieve perfection. All the men and women on television or movies seem to have flat stomachs and muscular bodies. If we're not careful we can begin to compare our spouses with those we see on television expect them to meet those standards. II Corinthians 10:12 says, *"For we dare not class ourselves or compare ourselves with those who commend themselves. But they measuring themselves by themselves, and comparing themselves among themselves, are not wise."*

Love your spouse for who they are and don't compare them to others. If you're around my age (late fifties) you've probably changed a lot physically and aren't likely to recapture the body you had when you were young. Still it's not a bad idea to develop a workout routine and do what you can to remain attractive for your mate. I realize that each person is free to enjoy television or movies based on their own convictions. I've personally made a decision to avoid movies that show sex scenes but not every Christian shares my opinion on this subject. I'm afraid of the images getting stuck in my head and interfering with the intimacy I enjoy with my wife. Perhaps even worse is the stimulation of unhealthy sexual fantasies. You must remember what you're seeing is acting and as my high school drama teacher would tell us, "Acting is bigger than life!" In other words the behavior you see is exaggerated! To expect that kind of activity from your spouse during lovemaking is unrealistic! Be very careful with how you handle social media, television, or movies because they can become huge distractions in your marriage and not only hinder your communication but your intimacy as well.

Chapter Six
Living with Fluid Boundaries
Balancing Marriage/Family and or Ministry

While I don't profess to be an expert on this particular subject it is my hope that I can share some insight that you may find helpful. One of the problems that I have struggled with over the years is establishing boundaries to ensure that I spend quality time with my wife and children. The problem is compounded by the fact that I've always been involved in the ministry of the church. And when I became the senior Pastor of the church in Washington, DC it became increasingly difficult. I realize that not everyone has those kinds of commitments in church but you may have other extracurricular activities that place demands your time. School activities or sports activities. Either way if you and your spouse work eight hours a day, five days a week, plus daily commuting time, and attend church regularly (two or three times a week), and have ministry involvement that requires your time on at least one non-church day, and have children participating in sports or school related activities that require your support, and have friends and family who regularly depend on you for help or counsel, you've got very little time left for your marriage.

I've heard it said that the average person will spend two thirds of their life with job related responsibilities. That means either at work or traveling to and from work. If that's true then we're left with one third of our lifetime to spend on other things. I've always found it interesting that we use the word "spend" in reference to time. Most often the word "spend" is attached to the idea of money. The difference is when I spend all of my money somehow I always get more and have the opportunity to start the spending process all over again. But with time there is only a certain amount God gives to each of us and when we spend it there is no more. With money we even have the ability to save some of it for a later date. With time we use the phrase "save time" but the truth is there's no such thing. We can't put time aside and use it later. The clock never stops or pauses. There are three things we can do with time, spend it, waste it, or value it! Ephesians 5:15-16 says, *"See then that you walk circumspectly, not as fools but as wise, redeeming the time, because the days are evil."* When you and I redeem time is when we value it.

I like to recycle so I save my aluminum cans and plastic water bottles in order to redeem them for cash. Those items along with others have a redemption value. Jesus Christ with His blood redeemed us in order that the full value of our lives might be realized but that is an entirely different message altogether! So I've said all that to say it's probably not a good idea to waste the time we have available to us. And with so much of our time being allotted to so many other things we need to protect the time we set aside for our marriage and family. This is where I ask the question, "What kind of boundaries do you set for quality time with your marriage and family?" There are two kinds of boundaries I'd like to consider, fluid or concrete.

Throughout the years, I've gotten myself in trouble with my wife and children because of having fluid boundaries when it comes to giving them my time. I was guilty of underestimating how valuable my time was to my family. My problem was that whenever someone or something needed to be rescheduled I chose to put off my wife and children in favor of giving that time to others. As a Pastor or Minister I always had some really good spiritual excuses for why I had to do it. Someone needs prayer, or counseling. Or someone needs my advice. Perhaps it's someone I've been meaning to connect with or I need to disciple. I'm sure you get the picture. The reality is there will always be outside demands on our time and I understand that as a Pastor or Minister my role is to serve God's people. That being said, I also realize that my wife and children are no less an important ministry and I have a huge responsibility to them. I've had to learn, sometimes painfully, that I must have a stronger commitment to the time I set aside for my wife and children. When I looked at the big picture I came to the conclusion that there is only a small amount of time for me to spend so it must be spent wisely. The boundaries I set around my family need to be concrete not fluid! When I say I'm going to be there for them, that's where I need to be

Let me say that I'm aware there are no absolutes. In other words there will be occasions in which you and your spouse may agree to reschedule personal time for the sake of others, and if so that's fine, but you can't make those decisions alone and not expect consequences and repercussions. I accept that as a husband and the head of the wife according to God's word, that places the responsibility squarely on my shoulders. Let's look at what the word of God says in Malachi 2:13-16, *"And this is the second thing you do: You cover the altar of the Lord with tears, with weeping and crying; so He does not regard the offering anymore, nor receive it with goodwill from your hands. Yet you say, 'For what reason?' Because the Lord has been witness between you and the wife of your youth, with whom you have dealt treacherously; yet she is your companion and your wife by covenant. But did He not make them one, having a remnant of the Spirit? And why one? He seeks godly offspring. Therefore take heed to your spirit, and let none deal treacherously with the wife of his youth. 'For the Lord God of Israel says that He hates divorce. For it covers one's garment with violence,' Says the Lord of hosts. Therefore take heed to your spirit, that you do not deal treacherously."*

As a preacher for over twenty five years I can honestly say that the book of Malachi has rarely if ever been used to teach on marriage and yet here it is! I would say that not giving the proper value to the time you've been given for your marriage is a treacherous practice. A practice that will cost you over the long haul. Husbands who neglect to spend an adequate amount of time investing in their marriage and family are treading on dangerous ground. Many extramarital affairs have been the result of such negligence. Continuing to break dates with your wife and children sends the message to them that you have other more important things to do than to be with them.

Shortly after I had taken over the church in Washington DC, my son Devon came to me one day and said, "Dad, every since we came here you don't have time for us anymore." It hurt me to hear him say that but he was absolutely right. I was so caught up in doing the work of the ministry I forgot that I had a ministry at home that needed some attention as well. Malachi 2:15 says, *"He seeks godly offspring."* How can I possibly accomplish that unless I prioritize the development of my children. My advice is to not take on extra responsibilities just to impress the Pastor or your boss. Maintain balance with your commitments and don't overextend yourself to the point that your marriage and family suffers. Set aside time for your wife and children and make those boundaries concrete not fluid. Do everything in your power to not break dates with your family unless you absolutely cannot avoid it. It will pay huge dividends for you and go a long way towards having a strong and healthy family atmosphere to come home to.

Chapter Seven
High Maintenance Couples vs. Low Maintenance Couples
Intellectual and Spiritual Compatibility

What makes two people compatible? Can a high maintenance personality co-exist with a low maintenance personality? Is it possible for two people whose intellectual and spiritual capacities are completely different to enjoy a happy union? How can two individuals know if they're compatible or not? My goal in this section is to hopefully bring some clarity to an issue that can be very troubling for a lot of couples who are either married or looking to get married. I'm not going to declare that I have all the answers to this problem because quite frankly I don't believe anyone can positively distinguish which two people are meant to be together based on personality but God Himself! Let's begin by examining what the word compatible means. Compatible – (1) two things able to exist or occur together without conflict.; (2) a computer that can use software designed for another make or type. I believe that those two definitions can go a long way in solving the question of compatibility.

Throughout my experiences in ministry I've known many Pastors who have fought to keep two individuals apart because they were convinced of their incompatibility only to see them get married and have successful marriages. The truth is I've also seen them be right and watched disaster unfold in those relationships. If you're reading this you may be thinking I'm contradicting what I said earlier about marriage being a reflection of the relationship between

Christ and the church. I did in fact say that Christ and the church were made for each other and that marriage is a divine union between two people who belong together. When those two people are operating within the will of God I absolutely believe that to be true.

But even two people walking with God who are ignorant regarding the divine arrangement they're participating in can allow what God put together to be torn apart. We must also consider II Corinthians 6:14 when it says we should *"not be unequally yoked together."* I know that verse speaks specifically about connecting with unbelievers but nevertheless the idea of being attached to wrong person is communicated. As is the case so many times in our lives God will lead us to the right situation but we still need to choose wisely. So it would seem that because of the free will God has given us we do have the capacity to make a bad choice. Having said all that I still believe that regardless of how the choice was made or the quality of that choice, once the vows have been exchanged the individuals involved are responsible to make whatever adjustments necessary to make the relationship work.

When I think of high maintenance personalities I consider the type of people who require a lot to keep them happy. They're usually the kind of people who get their happiness from external things rather than internal things. They generally need a lot of money, nice clothes, nice car, and a nice house in order for them to be happy. If you're married to a high maintenance person and you cannot deliver on most of these things you're marriage could be in jeopardy. But it doesn't stop at just the material things. Many high maintenance types also require an excessive amount of personal attention. Their egos may need to be stroked regularly as well as needing more reassurance than normal. They may place an unusually high demand on people around them to help keep them happy. Sometimes the smallest disappointment can send them into a state of depression. It's also not out of character for them to be overly concerned with maintaining a certain status around their peers.

On the positive side high maintenance people have high expectations for their children's standard of living. That usually translates into above average academic achievement which is always a good thing. It can also teach them to not settle for second best. They can also push or motivate their spouse to excel in life. If any or all of this describes either you or your spouse, one of you could have a high maintenance personality. That doesn't automatically spell doom for your relationship. It just means you know who you are or who you're married to. Some men don't have a problem keeping a high maintenance woman happy. Conversely some women don't have a problem keeping a high maintenance husband happy.

The low maintenance personality is generally the polar opposite of their counterpart. Low maintenance people get their happiness mostly from internal things rather than external. Like everyone else they like having money but they have the ability to find joy in the simple things. They're happy with a quiet and peaceful home. They probably dress modestly most of the time and are satisfied with a reliable car even if it isn't the nicest. Most of the time, they'll weather the financial storms of life without too much complaining. Certainly their loyalty to their spouse isn't dependent upon those material things. Low maintenance people are also more likely to not need constant reassurance of being loved, an occasional kiss, a hug, or a quiet evening together is usually sufficient. More often than not, they bounce back fairly quickly from disappointments. On the negative side they can be too passive in terms of having expectations for their children's futures. They can sometimes promote an attitude that says average is okay. They tend to settle and allow their spouses to do the same. If any or all of this describe either you or your spouse, you could have a low maintenance personality. Once again there's no cause for alarm. Many men and women have a low maintenance spouse and are extremely happy. I believe that two low maintenance people can be very happy as well as two high maintenance people. However, it seems to me that a combination of the two is probably best. I suggest that both parties can benefit from the positive attributes of the other.

The same can be said for intellectuals and spirituals. Maybe you're not the most spiritual person in the world. You may be more calculating and analytical. That can be a great asset to your marriage because there are times when situations need to be analyzed. Even if your spouse approaches everything with a spiritual mind sometimes rational thinking can bring balance and help stabilize the decision making process. You may say "but Pastor I need to act more in faith than in my own thinking," and you'd be right but make no mistake about it, faith is not ignorant. If you're an intellectual use it to study God's word so you can better understand how to apply your faith. If you're a spiritual person then you should pray for some balance in your approach to life because believe it or not, sometimes you do need to look before you leap!

The bottom line is compatibility isn't about being the same, it's about knowing how to blend two different personalities into something beautiful! So what if you and your spouse's thinking is contradictory, learn how to reap the benefits of your differing opinions. In II Peter 1:5 he says we need to *"add to our faith..."* which tells me that none of us are complete where we stand today. Maybe God has given you your mate for the purpose of addition but rather than allow it you've been wasting time on subtraction. Don't get caught up in trying to take away your spouse's God given virtues just so they can be like you. Value their uniqueness and take on the virtues you lack and the two of you can complete each other. I like the definition of compatibility that refers to a computer working with software from another make or type. That my friend is the type of compatibility we need to have an effective and flourishing marriage relationship! So who is compatible? Whoever chooses to be!

I would like to finish this section by discussing the compatibility of the believer with the unbeliever. Earlier in this chapter I referenced II Corinthians 6:14 where it says *"Do not be unequally yoked together with unbelievers."* That verse, at least as far as this discussion, is more applicable to a single Christian who wants to get married. The message is clear if you're a single Christian you should not marry an unbeliever. However if two people get married as unbelievers and only one becomes a Christian, that presents an entirely different set of circumstances. I Corinthians 7:12-

13 says, *"If any brother has a wife who does not believe, and she is willing to live with him, let him not divorce her. And a woman who has a husband who does not believe, if he is willing to live with her, let her not divorce him."* It would seem that even a believer and an unbeliever can be compatible depending upon the condition of the hearts of those involved. Certainly God makes it clear that having an unbelieving spouse is not grounds for divorce. In fact verse 16 says, *"For how do you know, O wife, whether you will save your husband? Or how do you know, O husband, whether you will save your wife?"* In these situations there always remains the possibility of seeing one's spouse converted. I suppose the only hindrance to accomplishing that goal would be the unwillingness to be a reflection of God's love for your spouse.

So it would appear that compatibility at its core is about the condition of the heart. If we yield our hearts to the Lord and become more Christ-like in our behavior we can learn to be compatible with the person we joined ourselves to in marriage. We should vow today to co-exist with our wives or husbands in love and peace and bring honor and glory to the Lord with our marriages.

Chapter Eight
Sex and Its Importance in Marriage

When it comes to sex and Christianity it can almost feel like they don't belong together. I've had several experiences with teaching about marriage in churches in which the members became very uncomfortable when the subject of sex was addressed. And if the truth is told, early in my walk with God I was uncomfortable talking about it as well. It was largely because of my limited knowledge of God and His word that I was unable to reconcile sex and spirituality.

I was in Aucklund, New Zealand teaching a marriage class and when I started to discuss sex the looks on their faces were priceless. When I looked around at all the children running around in the church I thought to myself, "Surely they're familiar with the concept!" There was so much embarrassment and awkwardness in the atmosphere that I started to feel uneasy and thought about changing the subject but I didn't because I understand the necessity of educating God's people so they can enjoy healthy and productive marriages. I do take into consideration that there are some saints who are old fashioned and believe this is not a topic of discussion that belongs in the church but rather needs to be addressed in the privacy of the home. The problem I see with that line of thinking is that most couples struggle in the area of communication and are not likely to talk about it. So then if there's frustration at home regarding sex and it's not communicated openly it could possibly lead to infidelity.

When the bible says in Matthew 19:5, *"For this reason a man shall leave his father and mother and be joined to his wife, and the two shall become one flesh,"* it is referencing the consummation of marriage through the sexual relationship enjoyed by husband and wife. The bible also says in II Corinthians 6:16-17, *"Or do you not know that he who is joined to a harlot is one body with her? For 'the two,' He says, 'shall become one flesh.' But he who is joined to the Lord is one spirit with him."* This takes us back to the fundamental truth that marriage is a reflection of the relationship between Christ and the church. If being joined to the Lord makes us one spirit with Him then being joined to our spouse makes us one spirit with each other.

There appears to be more than just a physical connection that occurs through sex but also a connection of soul and spirit as well. With that in mind it makes sense that marriage is what God joined together and what man should not separate. Marriage is then a holy union established by God and intended to be a preview of His love for us. It was designed to be a lifelong commitment between two people that would ultimately produce the godly offspring He desires. This is also why adultery is immoral. A man cannot become one with two women nor can a woman become one with two men. A marriage requires a 100% commitment to each other and it's not possible to give 100% of one's self to two different people. Adultery corrupts the purity of the spiritual connection between husband and wife and is given as a justifiable reason for divorce. Keep in mind that God says that because of adultery one CAN divorce, not that one MUST divorce. Even marriages damaged by infidelity can still experience reconciliation and healing because with God nothing is impossible! If the Agape love of God is flowing through us we can overcome any obstacle in our way!

So, where does sex rank in terms of the most important things in marriage? I suppose it depends on many contributing factors. Age can play a major role in answering that question for some couples. If you're a young couple in your twenties of thirties, there should be fireworks going off in your bedroom regularly. Even in your forties and fifties without any health concerns that would limit your productivity you should be doing alright. Obviously as we get a little older there will naturally be some slowing down but again without any major health concerns many couples are active sexually right up till the end! Personally I'd like to think that's gonna be me and my wife!

Regardless of our age we must be attentive to the sexual needs of our spouse. Being negligent in this area of our relationships is a bad practice that will eventually lead to problems. Stress can also play a role in answering that question for some couples. A high stress level in the household can absolutely have a negative impact on our sex lives. Some people react to stress differently than others. If you're faith is not at the place where you can manage your stress it can knock the romance right out of you. With the high cost of living these days it's easy for a couple to feel overwhelmed while trying to afford housing, transportation, and raising a family. That pressure can cause stress, and that stress can cause us to lose focus on building our marriage relationships. If your stress levels are out of control you would be wise to find some stress relieving activities. (Now that I think about it, sex is a pretty good stress reliever if you ask me!) But seriously, it could be sports or exercise or anything that frees your mind.

Of course, the best method to use as a stress reliever is prayer. Never underestimate the power of prayer to help you cope with life's challenges. When it's all said and done if your spouse feels neglected in the bedroom and you use stress as an excuse for your failure to perform, it may not sit well with them because everyone is battling with stress to some degree. Another issue that can play a role in answering that question is health. There's no denying that a debilitating health condition can restrict one's ability to maintain a strong and consistent sex life. Depending on the severity of the condition it could conceivably spell the end of one's ability to have sex altogether. If a health problem limits or restricts your mate in the area of sexual performance, clearly sex has to take on a lesser role in your marriage. It is in these situations where the full force and power of the vows we made must be applied. We all declared that we would remain together in sickness and in health. Sadly, for some couples their relationship will be tested in the area of sickness. If this happens in your marriage then it's inevitable that sex must take a back seat to the more important matter of taking care of your spouse and providing them with the loyalty and emotional support they need.

So what are some suggestions for ways to keep the fire burning in the bedroom? Let's first look at what the bible says about it. Hebrews 13:4 says, *"Marriage is honorable among all, and the bed undefiled;"* We see the writer of the book of Hebrews clearing up any discrepancies we might have about the bible and sex. My wife and I just celebrated our 29th Wedding Anniversary recently, and we were together for 10 years prior to getting married. So we have a 39 year relationship that needs our care and attention so it doesn't grow stale and boring. Anyone who's been with their spouse that long or longer understands that there is very little mystery left in the relationship so creativity becomes imperative. I have to be honest that takes a lot of work for me because I am admittedly not the most romantic man in the world. I like sports and enjoy action movies, preferably sci-fi action. If the movie doesn't include guns, explosions, fights, car chases and everything associated with those kinds of movies, I'm probably not interested. I abhor chick flicks! When I tell my wife I'm trying to get in touch with my feminine side she says I don't have one.

But I do work at being more romantic so I can make my wife happy. We've done a lot of things together that have helped to keep our nights hot and sexy! Occasionally I've gotten us a hotel room for a night even without leaving town. The sole purpose was to be together, not necessarily get away. Those times have always been a lot of fun! I've also tried to work on romancing her all day and not just at night. Too often we as men want to just tap her on the shoulder late at night and say "let's go!" and half an hour later (If she's lucky!) we're asleep. I will sometimes start sending her sexy messages early in the day. I guess the kids call it "sexting". It may not work for everyone but it has made for some really exciting nights for us. Some days it's just a little playful touching that happens during the day to let her know I'm thinking about her. I'll even break out some of my old pick-up lines on her every now and then. They're corny and usually make her laugh but I still get the desired result.

As a husband you need to do all you can to not be a microwave lover! Some men are finished so fast their wives are still trying to figure out if something even happened. Don't be so selfish that your only concern is satisfying your own needs and not hers. I also do the best I can to maintain my appearance so that she still finds me attractive. It's important to do all the little things you can to show your spouse you still find them sexy and desirable. Especially as we age and start to lose our youthful looks. Let's face it with age comes loss of hair for some, loss of teeth, what hair is left is now gray, and on top of the years we're gaining - we gain weight! I believe that women particularly need to have their beauty and attractiveness affirmed by their husbands. My advice to the women is to think like a man sometimes and initiate the action! I guarantee you your husband will love it! There is so much more you can do as a couple to stimulate excitement and enthusiasm in your sex life! You're only limited by your own imagination and creativity!

As a final word on this very important matter let's go back to the word of God and see what else the bible says about sexual activity in marriage. In II Corinthians chapter 7 we see that the word instructs us to maintain consistency in the area of intimacy. II Corinthians 7:2-5 says, *"Nevertheless, because of sexual immorality, let each man have his own wife, and let each woman have her own husband. Let the husband render to his wife the affection due her, and likewise the wife also to the husband. The wife does not have authority over her own body, but the husband does. And likewise the husband does not have authority over his own body, but the wife does. Do not deprive one another except with consent for a time, that you may give yourselves to fasting and prayer; and come together again so that Satan does not tempt you because of your lack of self control."* We are taught that withholding sex from our spouse should only happen by mutual agreement and the motivation for doing so should be of a spiritual nature, not anger or as a way of punishing our mate. The bible is also saying that regular sexual activity in a marriage can be a prophylactic against adultery or sexual immorality. I believe if every married couple were to apply these verses to their relationships it would go a long way toward building happy marriages!

Chapter Nine
Is the Husband the Head?

What does the bible mean when it says the husband is the head of the wife? Is it saying the husband is the boss or ruler over his wife? Does it give the husband the right to have her at his disposal to serve his every need? There is probably a lot of confusion about how one is to interpret what God is saying when He declares the husband to be the head. Over the years I've always encountered people who say, "There's many ways to interpret the bible!" and they're absolutely right! The problem is that only one of those ways is accurate. I'm under no illusion by thinking there won't be individuals who will disagree with my evaluation of this subject and that's okay with me. My prayer is that at the very least it will stimulate some healthy discussion about how we as men are to live this out in our marriages. Ephesians 5:23-24 says, *"For the husband is the head of the wife, as also Christ is the head of the church; and He is the Savior of the body. Therefore, just as the church is subject to Christ, so let the wives be to their own husbands in everything."*

What most men will see is that they have a God-given right to be in charge when it comes to what their wife should or shouldn't do. So often I've heard men say, "My wife won't listen to me!" or "My wife won't submit to my authority as a man!" and in my opinion they're only half right in their thinking. Should the wife listen to her husband? Yes! Should the wife submit to her husband's authority? Yes! But as it was mentioned in chapter three, marriage is about love and respect! The bible says to the women in Ephesians 5:33, *"and let the wife see that she respects her husband."* One thing I do know about respect and that is that it's earned, not given. If the man approaches his wife armed with that information he will be more likely to get the result he's looking for.

What the world needs are more men who are full of God's Spirit! Marriages would be a lot stronger with husbands who bear the fruit of the Spirit in their relationship with their wives. I would like to draw your attention to a familiar passage of scripture that doesn't always come up when discussing the subject of marriage. The passage I'm referencing is Galatians 5:22-23 where the Apostle Paul details the fruit of the Spirit. *"But the fruit of the Spirit is love, joy, peace, longsuffering, kindness, goodness, faithfulness, gentleness, self-control. Against such there is no law."* What must not be missed is that all of these actions are described as "fruit" that are a by-product of being filled with God's Spirit. When I was in school as a boy I recall being taught that the difference between a fruit and a vegetable is seed. Notice that it isn't called the "vegetable" of the Spirit, but it is the "fruit" because of the seed! In Genesis 1:11 the bible says, *"Then God said, 'Let the earth bring forth grass, the herb that yields seed, and the fruit tree that yields fruit according to its kind, whose seed is in itself, on the earth' and it was so."*

God has always intended for man to lead and rule. But God also made man responsible for the productivity of what He placed him over. As man was given responsibility for the productivity of the garden, even so man was given responsibility for the productivity of his marriage. As a husband I'm responsible to bear the fruit of the Spirit in my marital relationship. When the fruit of love is in my marriage, there is a seed inside of it capable of producing more love. When the fruit of joy is in my marriage, there is a seed inside of it capable of producing more joy. Can you see where this is going? This is not to say that the wife doesn't bear fruit! But the wife's fruit will always be proportionate to the fruit the man has sown into his marriage. She is not the head, the man is! So that means everything starts and ends with the man! If I haven't sown kindness, there's a pretty good chance I won't grow any. The husband is the tree that yields fruit according to its kind! What kind of fruit is growing in your marriage man of God? Or maybe I should ask is there any fruit growing in your marriage? The fruit, "whose seed is in itself," will reproduce in your relationship! It has to because it operates on principle!

Of course, there are situations in which the man concedes his position as the tree and the woman assumes leadership and attempts to do the sowing. It usually doesn't work because it's out of order with how God established it to be! If we go back to the preceding verses in Galatians chapter five we see the opposite end of the spectrum. In verses 19-21 the bible says, *"Now the works of the flesh are evident, which are: adultery, fornication, uncleanness, lewdness, idolatry, sorcery, hatred, contentions, jealousies, outbursts of wrath, selfish ambitions, dissensions, heresies, envy, murders, drunkenness, revelries, and the like;"* Because the fruit of the Spirit is listed as a contrast to the works of the flesh, I'm going to refer to them as the "fruit" of the flesh for the sake of argument. Jesus said in Matthew 7:17-18, *"Even so, every good tree bears good fruit, but a bad tree bears bad fruit. A good tree cannot bear bad fruit, nor can a bad tree bear good fruit."* If we follow that line of thinking it's safe to say there is such a thing as bad fruit. However it would still carry seed because it is a fruit. If the man or woman is not filled with the Holy Spirit there is only one kind of fruit they can produce, and that would be bad fruit. And if that fruit carries seed then it is conceivable that one could sow the "fruit" of the flesh into one's marriage. Like it says in Galatians 6:7, *"...for whatever a man sows, that he will also reap."*

Let's look at it another way. I'm a huge sports fan! I enjoy basketball, football, baseball, boxing, track, and many other activities that involve competition. What I've noticed throughout the years as I've followed various college and professional team sports is that when a team doesn't perform at the level of expectation placed on them by upper management they usually fire the coach. Even though he never dropped a touchdown pass, threw an interception, missed a basket, or struck out with the bases loaded, he or she always carries the responsibility for the team's failure and success. Being the coach of the team means being the head of the team. While a team is under the leadership of a specific coach, he/she is statistically responsible for all their wins and losses. When the team wins a championship the coach is celebrated as a champion and the players are said to have benefitted from his/her leadership. My point is obvious, the coach is the head and must take the blame for the productivity of the team whether it's good, bad, or mediocre, the responsibility falls squarely on the coaches' shoulders.

So I ask you husband, are you the head? Are you willing to carry the burden that comes with being the head?

Are you and your wife as a team winning or losing? What kind of fruit would God find in your marriage today? One day I woke up and realized there was a whole lot more involved in being the head than I had considered. I'm aware that this can sound like the wife is being let off the hook when it comes to her contribution to the relationship but nothing could be further from the truth. She is still responsible to respect her husband's role as the head and remember that when he wins, she wins. She must cheer him on and give him the support he needs to fulfill his God-given assignment in life. The wife would also do well to remember that the two have indeed become one and she should do all she can to become a team player. Without cooperation from the wife the husband is assured of failure. My advice then is to stay in your lane and know your role! And if you get out of your lane, slow your roll! Just make sure husbands that you understand what it means to be the head of the wife and do everything within your power to fulfill your responsibilities.

Chapter Ten
Is Divorce an Option for the Christian Marriage?

There is no question that this is a sore subject in the church and one that most Pastors would just as soon avoid. This for some will turn out to be the most unpopular chapter in the book. Some will ask why I would include such information when it contradicts everything we believe. First of all, I'm a firm believer that people should be educated in all facets of life. Why should we leave it up to the secular world to teach our people when it's within our power to do so? And secondly, I'm not sure it contradicts what we believe at all. All I'm going to say is what the bible says and if a Pastor or leader has a problem with that then they should take it up with the Lord.

Let me make it clear that my feelings are that divorce shouldn't be an option. But even though I feel like it shouldn't be an option the bible disagrees with me and does give believers permission under certain circumstances. Let me also make this clear, the bible in no way suggests or recommends divorce, it simply states that it CAN be done. Let's look at what the bible says in Matthew 19:7-8, *"They said to Him, 'Why then did Moses command to give a certificate of divorce, and to put her away?' He said to them, 'Moses, because of the hardness of your hearts, permitted you to divorce your wives, but from the beginning it was not so. And I say to you, whoever divorces his wife, except for sexual immorality, and marries another, commits adultery; and whoever marries her who is divorced commits adultery.'"*

When the word says, "but from the beginning it was not so." It shows us that God has been and is always against divorce because He is the God who does not change. He's the same yesterday, today and forever! (Hebrews 13:8)

The part that causes me to constantly examine myself is when he says "because of the hardness of your hearts." Here is a picture of the stubbornness and rebelliousness of mankind. He's saying if your hearts were not so hard you would be able to overcome anything and stay together. Here I must echo what was said earlier about marriage being a reflection of the relationship between Christ and the church. When I take that into consideration I'm glad that in spite of my sometimes adulterous behavior the Lord will never divorce me! Let's be honest we're all guilty at times of having a divided heart when it comes to our loyalty to God and yet His love never fails! Ezekiel 6:9 says, *"Then those of you who escape will remember Me among the nations where they are carried, because I was crushed by their adulterous heart which has departed from Me, and by their eyes which play the harlot after their idols; they will loathe themselves for the evils which they committed in all their abominations."* This is a passage that brings conviction to my life when God says He is crushed by our adulterous hearts and our eyes that play the harlot after idols. And yet He still doesn't divorce us! The love of God overcomes our adultery but He says our hearts are too hard to overcome it with our spouses. I'm not suggesting that adultery is an easy thing to overcome but with God all things are possible!

The problem that many couples face today is the bible only lists adultery as a legitimate reason for divorcing while they're experiencing domestic violence or a spouse who abuses their children physically or maybe even sexually, or other crimes that are not addressed in the scriptures. What advice can be given to the person who is being victimized by crimes of this nature? As a Pastor I have never advised anyone to divorce regardless of the circumstances although I have at times felt like it. What position can a believer take when they're being terrorized in their own homes by a violent spouse while trying to be obedient to God regarding their marriage? While the bible doesn't speak specifically to those issues, I believe it does lead us in the right direction regarding answers to tough questions like that. Let's take a look at Romans 13:1-4, *"Let every soul be subject to the governing authorities. For there is no authority except from God, and the authorities that exist are appointed by God. Therefore whoever resists the authority resists the ordinance of God, and those who resist will bring judgment on themselves. For rulers are not a terror to good works, but to evil. Do you want to be unafraid of the authority? Do what is good, and you will have praise from the same. For he is God's minister to you for good. But if you do evil, be afraid; for he does not bear the sword in vain; for he is God's minister, an avenger to execute wrath on him who practices evil."*

Here we find the word of God teaching about law and government. It is specifically teaching about how we are to interact with the local authorities or police. If you're from the inner-city like me it's likely that this is an uncomfortable relationship for you. As a young person running the streets we didn't exactly have a love relationship with the police. We were always taught to never tell the police anything or "snitches get stitches" or something along those lines. Many couples who were raised in the inner-city carry that mentality into their marriages and would rather endure abuse than see their spouse incarcerated.

I have, for the past several years, been on a bible reading schedule that allows me to read the entire bible from cover to cover every year. I imagine that I've probably read the bible close to ten times over the last seven years or so. The theme that's hard to miss, especially when you read the books of the prophets, is God's concern for people to receive justice. He constantly uses the prophets to speak out against the injustices of society. The prophets weren't exactly community activists but they were the voice of God for the people who suffered injustices. While it is true that much of that injustice was being committed by the governing bodies, He was still concerned about the fair and just treatment of His people.

I'm not trying to open a discussion about government or police corruption, because that would be missing the point entirely. The point is that there are laws in place to protect people from being victimized by violence and crime. It's also important to take note that the only instances in which God's people broke the law without sinning is when the laws of man asked them to violate the laws of God. In the book of Acts chapter 4, Peter and John were told by the Sanhedrin (a group of men comprised of Pharisees and Sadducees) that they were not to speak anymore in the name of Jesus. Peter responded in verses 19-20 by saying, *"Whether it is right in the sight of God to listen to you more than God, you judge. For we cannot but speak the things which we have seen and heard."* So if the law doesn't ask us to break the commandments of God we're obligated to obey the law.

There are laws to protect us against acts of violence and those laws are no less significant when the violence occurs within the confines of a marriage relationship. I have, by the grace of God, never put my hands on my wife regardless of what we were dealing with and I believe that any husband who uses violence against his wife, should be held accountable. However, I also believe that if there is genuine repentance the relationship can be salvaged. When I say genuine repentance I mean a 180 degree turn from that sin so that it never happens again. Not an apology that comes with crocodile tears only to see the same behavior resurface a week or two later. And any behavior that endangers children must be met with an immediate and forceful response for their protection, not the protection of the person responsible. Jesus says in Matthew 23:23, *"Woe to you, scribes and Pharisees, hypocrites! For you pay tithe of mint and anise and cumin, and have neglected the weightier matters of the law: justice and mercy and faith. These you ought to have done, without leaving the others undone."* He essentially tells them that their faithfulness in giving did not supersede the fact that they were responsible to live by the laws of justice, mercy and faith. So even a Christian who goes to church regularly and pays their tithes are still considered hypocrites if they're not practicing justice and mercy!

There are those who will read this chapter and say, "Hey Pastor, these things shouldn't be happening in the church!" My response is, "You're absolutely right! But they do happen in the church!" Throughout the world churches are seeing men and women from the inner-cities who come from lifestyles of addiction, crime, and violence become members of their congregations. Many of those people get married without being completely free from the behaviors of their past life and struggle in their family relationships. Also there are those who get married without seeking counsel from the leadership of the church and find themselves connected to someone about whose past they were ignorant. Those situations can sometimes lead to serious family tragedy.

So what am I saying with all this? I'm saying that the bible makes it clear that God's heart is against divorce! Malachi 2:16 says, *"For the Lord God of Israel says that He hates divorce, for it covers one's garment with violence."* It is His desire that couples make it together for life! God's will is for husbands to love their wives as Christ loves the church and in return his wife will respect him and they'll enjoy a beautiful life together. But I also acknowledge that there are unique situations that require extreme measures to be taken if the marriage is to survive. My prayer is that no wife or child would have to suffer abuse in their own home. My advice will always be the same. Work it out! Do all you can to save your marriage! If you need counseling, get it! Make every effort! Make every sacrifice! And when it's all said and done, be at peace with whatever decision you ultimately make knowing that the bible says in Romans 14:12, *"So then each of us shall give account of himself to God."* For God sees everything that's done on every high hill, and under every green tree!

Chapter Eleven
Till Death do Us Part!

What a profound statement we make during our vows when we repeat those words, "till death do us part." I believe for most people, the majority of what's said during the wedding ceremony is more or less just part of the program or just a formality. I can honestly say that when my wife and I exchanged our vows I really didn't comprehend the gravity or weight of the words we were speaking to one another. I mean the real significance of the spiritual experience we were having completely escaped me. I suppose the fact that I wasn't living right with God at the time contributed to my mentality. We're hoping that August 13, 2017 on our 30th Anniversary we can renew our vows and have the church wedding we never had! What I know now as opposed to what I knew then is as different as night and day! Even though I entered the marriage with limited understanding of what God truly wanted for me as a husband, we still managed to stay together all these years.

The older I get the more thankful I am for the partnership and friendship we've enjoyed for almost 40 years now. My wife Neissi has blessed me with three beautiful children, two sons, Chuck Jr. & Devon, with the potential to carry on the Turner family name, and one daughter, Cyndal, who I've always said is the one who makes my heart smile. When two people value each other and honor the commitment they've made before God, it can make for an awesome life experience. God, through His word makes it clear that the only thing that should separate a husband and wife is death itself which is also the separation of soul and spirit from the body. The truth is we all at some point will exit this life in our bodily form and our soul and spirit will enter into eternity with Christ if we're born again believers. It is this reality that should motivate us to live out our marriage commitment before the world as a demonstration of the love of Christ! My goal is to love and cherish my spouse for as many years as the Lord gives us here on earth.

From what I understand in the word of God the relationship we enjoy with our spouses will not continue in the resurrection so we would be wise to make the most of it. Let's take a look at Matthew 22:23-30, *'The same day the Sadducees, who say there is no resurrection, came to Him, and asked Him, saying, "Teacher, Moses said that if a man dies, having no children, his brother shall marry his wife and raise up offspring for his brother. Now there were with us seven brothers. The first died after he had married, and having no offspring, left his wife to his brother. Likewise the second also, and the third, even to the seventh. Last of all the woman died also. Therefore, in the resurrection, whose wife of the seven will she be? For they all had her."* Jesus answered and said to them, *"You are mistaken, not knowing the Scriptures nor the power of God. For in the resurrection they neither marry nor are they given in marriage, but are like angels of God in heaven."*

So it would seem that what God joins together no man is to separate, but in the resurrection God himself does the separating. Some may find this a little discouraging but it's what the word of God says. We do re-marry in the resurrection as the church who is the bride of Christ! But this marriage will be spiritual, not physical. I'd be lying if I said that I didn't wish that My wife and I could continue our relationship in heaven but based on what the Scripture teaches, that wouldn't make sense. Since we are as the body of believers, the bride of Christ, and enter into a marriage relationship with Him, we can't also be married to our earthly spouses or that would equate to bigamy. We can all look forward to a glorious eternity with Jesus in which our love and loyalty will be to Him and Him alone! The bible teaches in I Corinthians 7:32-34 that those who are married have their loyalty divided between the Lord and their spouse. It is absolutely true that as a married man, even as a man of God, I must strive to balance my love for God with my love for my wife, all the while knowing I cannot neglect either of them.

Jesus told the Sadducees they didn't know the power of God and in many ways we don't know His power either! I don't truly understand how God is going to separate me and my wife in the resurrection but I know based on the word of God that I won't be unhappy about it! I could speculate that we will recognize each other but not inter-relate the same way we did on earth. I'm only speculating but on the Mount of Transfiguration Peter, James and John did recognize Moses and Elijah. I'm not sure that's an indicator but if it is it would seem that in the resurrection we'll recognize each other.

I pray that brings some comfort to those who perhaps were hoping to continue their relationships in heaven in the same manner in which we enjoyed them here on earth. Here's what I do believe, the promise of eternity and the life we'll have on the other side will far exceed anything we've ever experienced. Even though as we say in our vows, "till death do us part" evidently death truly will part us. But be encouraged for the bible says in I Corinthians 2:9 *"But as it is written: 'Eye has not seen, nor ear heard, nor have entered into the heart of man the things which God has prepared for those who love Him."* It also says in Revelation 21:4, *"And God will wipe away every tear from their eyes; there shall be no more death, nor sorrow, nor crying. There shall be no more pain, for the former things have passed away."* With or without my wife, that sounds like a pretty good deal to me. But as I mentioned earlier all this does is encourage me even more to enjoy my wife and love her as best I can for this is the life that God has given us together! What kind of life will she and I have together in heaven? Obviously no one can say with absolute certainty. But suffice it to say it will be gloriously different, definitely not bad. Gloriously different!

Chapter Twelve
A Final Word

As I close this book let me first acknowledge that there is so much more that could be said about marriage. It's a subject whose depth I'm not sure anyone can completely explore and expose. But I've tried to share what I believe to be the issues that have been most prevalent during the many times I have counseled with married couples over the years. It was not my goal to psycho-analyze couples in order to give them a clinical diagnosis of their problems but rather to offer a biblical perspective that shares God's heart for marriages. Hopefully the information will be both practical and applicable for some who are experiencing marital struggles. If it was your goal to find some undiscovered secret that would instantaneously transform your marriage into a magical and romantic journey that lasts a lifetime, you're probably still searching. Don't let anyone fool you there are no quick fixes, no magic scriptures, and no automatic answers. The scripture has the power to transform your marriage but only so much as you and I are willing to apply its truth to our relationships. So what is the revelation that we need to live in victory with our spouses? It is that building a successful marriage is hard work! I know that's really not revelation, its information at best. But sometimes for the person who is battling to save their marriage the simplest answer can be the one that causes a light to click on in their heads and change the destiny of their relationship.

Hopefully we can agree that it takes **Destiny & Courage** to develop a marriage where two people are thriving and not just surviving. I believe that the bible clearly teaches that God's desire for married couples is that they would stick together through thick and thin by overcoming every obstacle the enemy puts in their path. The bible teaches in two ways, explicitly and implicitly. When we read, *"You shall not steal."* (Exodus 20:15) it is explicit or stated clearly and leaves no room for doubt. However, when we read, *"Be holy, for I am holy."* (I Peter 1:16) it is implicit or implied though not plainly expressed. The verse about stealing is easily interpreted and no one can argue the meaning while the verse about holiness, although clear to me, will leave some people room to question the meaning of the command. I believe it's because many Christians reject the implicit teaching of the bible that we have so many in the church who smoke cigarettes, or drink alcohol, or use drugs, because they're looking for an explicit command and ignoring what the bible implies as truth. To suggest the word of God doesn't teach against smoking or addictions because it isn't explicitly mentioned is to be ignorant of the implicit truths found in the bible.

My point is that the bible teaches both ways about marriage and if you and I take the time to read the scriptures we'll find all the answers we need for how to inter-relate with our mates. As a follower of Christ my behavior often comes down to simple choices of right and wrong. I suggest that more often than not the truth is black and white, not the gray areas we're so quick to choose. The bible makes it very clear in James 4:17 when it says, *"Therefore, to him who knows to good and does not do it, to him it is sin."* That's about as explicit as it gets! The bottom line is husbands, do good to your wife! And wife, do good to your husband!

I suppose if I had to choose one piece of advice to leave with other couples it would be to build your marriage on the strength of friendship! It has been my experience that when the husband and wife are not just lovers but best friends, the chances for success increase dramatically! When I was a young man I struggled to give up spending most of my free time with my male friends but as I've matured it has become more and more enjoyable to spend the majority of my free time with my spouse. The reward for choosing to be with my wife more is that we've grown to know each other far more intimately than we had in the past. We're able to share openly and honestly about our joys and our sorrows, our victories and disappointments, our struggles and our victories! A strong friendship will breed open communication. The kind of communication that isn't superficial or as one writer called it, "elevator talk". Most people don't talk at all in an elevator, and when they do it's usually about the weather or something shallow just to pass time until they reach their desired floor. A good marriage cannot survive on "elevator talk" it takes conversations with depth and substance to build a bond that lasts a lifetime.

That means as men we sometimes have to put aside our pride and risk being vulnerable with the woman we love. My wife (Neissi) doesn't enjoy all of things I enjoy, especially sports, but she allows me to watch games because she knows it means something to me and I really do appreciate it. I'm not always in the mood for the crime dramas she likes but I watch them with her because I know it means something to her. And every now and then I'll even suffer through a "chick flick" (although I must admit that it's very rare) because I know she enjoys movies that make her cry. Personally I like car chases, explosions, and fights, lots of fights! Never mind that the plot is predictable, just give me action!

I say all that to say my wife and I are best friends! We go for walks together. We take long drives together. One of the most awesome trips we ever took was driving from Washington, DC to California together. It was just the two of us for six days spending quality time with each other. If you haven't already done it, learn to become best friends with your spouse, you'll never live to regret it! Get to know each other deeply and intimately! Kiss each other passionately! Hug like you haven't seen each other in weeks! And don't forget how important it is to make each other laugh! A great sense of humor can be a powerful stress reliever in these tough days we're living in.

And lastly, if you have children let your marriage bring stability to their lives. A peaceful household can contribute greatly to your children's attitude and behavior at home, at school, and in the community where they live. Certainly this isn't new information but it's worth repeating. I would also advise that fathers play a significant role in the lives of their daughters. Many men will take on the approach that says, "Let the mother raise the girls, and I'll raise the boys!" The problem with that thinking is that it ignores just how much little girls need their fathers influence. I believe that girls crave love and attention from a male, usually an authoritative male, and who better than the father to fill that role. I have always been very close to my daughter and continue to be close with her to this day at the age of 26. It is through the relationship with the father that girls learn to receive love and attention from a male in a non-sexual way. In a similar way to how wives prioritize love and attention over sex is how I believe girls need love and attention. When the father is constantly reminding his daughter how beautiful she is and showing her how much he cares for her by being there for her, she's less likely to be susceptible when a boy tells her she can only show or experience love through sex. So maybe, just maybe, the father can help prevent teenage pregnancy with his daughter. Obviously no method is 100% guaranteed to work but if you ask me it's the best approach you can take as a father.

When it came to raising my boys I actually found the job even more challenging. They needed to see me love and respect their mother so hopefully they would in turn learn to respect women. I was sometimes in conflict while trying to raise godly young men. The spiritual man wanted them to be non-violent at all costs. But the natural man who grew up in the inner-city wanted them to know how to defend themselves in a fight. I wanted them to be good Christian young men but I also didn't want them to get "punked" by any of the other boys. I remember the first time one of my sons gave a little boy a bloody nose, part of me wanted to rebuke him for fighting, while the other part of me wanted to give him a fist bump and proudly proclaim him to be a "chip off the old block!" It was easy for me to take a stand against premarital sex with my daughter, but with my sons I sometimes felt like congratulating them. Many of us as men wrestle with these same feelings while trying to raise our children the right way. I tried to find balance with my sons and teach them to only resort to violence as a means of defending themselves. I also, in spite of my pride and my flesh, tried to teach them to wait until after marriage to get involved sexually.

By the grace of God and the power of the Holy Spirit I pray that my marriage has been a reflection of the relationship between Christ and the church before my children. My kids are all grown up now and they're doing okay. Have they done all the things I would've wanted them to do? No, but they're doing okay. I was talking to my youngest son a couple months ago and he was telling me how much he appreciated how he'd always seen me treat his mother while they were growing up. He talked about never seeing us fighting or arguing. It has done my soul good to know that we've modeled a godly marriage in the eyes of our children. It's one thing for the people at church to think you have a good marriage. It's far more important for the people who live with you every day and see you at your best and worst to say it! So allow the Spirit of God and the love of Jesus Christ to saturate your marriage and family and I guarantee you'll be pleased with the outcome! Learn to cooperate with God's plan of **Destiny and Courage** for you and your spouse! Because when it's all said and done, if you're going to have a successful marriage, you're going to need to have a little **Destiny and Courage** in you!

32187207R00044

Made in the USA
Middletown, DE
08 January 2019